Edify and Encourage

Edify and Encourage

By

Missy Ducharme

COPYRIGHT

Printed in the United States of America by Ingramspark

First Printing, **January 2021**

ISBN **978-1-7362146-1-9 Print**

JEBWizard Publishing
37 Park Forest Rd,
Cranston, RI 02920
www.jebwizardpublishing.com

DEDICATION

This book is dedicated to Daniel, the man I love who inspires me every day. Thank you for your love and support and for sharing our love for Christ together.

Thank you to my daughter Juliet for your patience and for being the best daughter ever. Thank you to my daughter Emma Rose in heaven. You lead me closer to Christ every day and showed me how to love in ways unimaginable. Thank you to my parents, who raised me as a Christian and led and encouraged me every step of the way.

Thank you to all of my family and friends for unending support. Thank you to John and Robert for teaching me to be a better writer. Thank you, Joyce Meyer, for inspiring me to reach beyond what I thought was possible. Each of you has made it possible for me to live my dreams, and I am grateful for you all.

January

January 1

Your words are my joy and my hearts delight.

Jeremiah 15:16

We are called to the home of Christ. It is our responsibility as Christians to speak His word. It brings him great joy when you bring others closer and help them to know Him better. He takes care of those who love Him.

January 2

He fills my life with good things so that I stay young and

strong like an eagle.

Psalm 103:5

When we fill our lives with the Lord, He keeps us youthful and gives us

strength. The Spirit refreshes our soul so that we are ready to minister

to others, and we are prepared to fly.

January 3

A friend loves at all times.

Proverbs 17:17

God sends us friends that are like family. Someone who will stick by us

through the

good times and bad. A true friend will never leave you.

January 4

Arise, shine, for thy light is come, and the glory of the

Lord is risen upon thee.

Isaiah 60:1

This is a call to action. Let Jesus' light that is dwelling within you shine

through. Jesus is the light of the world. Rise up!

January 5

Blessed are the pure of heart: For they shall see God.

Matthew 5:8

God knows our hearts. When our hearts are pure, we will not only see

him in faith, we will see Him in heaven when our time has come.

January 6

With God, all things are possible.

Matthew 19:6

Anyone can be saved. We have to put God above all things. We cannot make things happen on our own, but the possibilities are endless with God in our lives.

January 7

Trust in the Lord with all of your heart and lean not on your own understanding; In all your ways acknowledge Him, and He shall direct thy paths.

Proverbs 3:5-6

Listen. Obey. You may not fully understand what He is asking you to do, but your devotion to Him will lead you to exactly where you are supposed to be. Then, when you get there, give Him all the glory.

January 8

Oh give thanks to the Lord for He is good! For His

mercies endure forever.

Psalm 107:1

He paid for our sins for the rest of our lives. It is important to be

grateful and give Him praise in all we do. Because of Him we are saved.

January 9

Ask and it will be given to you, seek, and you will find:

Knock and it will be opened to you.

Matthew 7:7

Prayer is our conversations with God. It is not only about what we are

seeking for ourselves. We must start with adoration, include

thanksgiving, and confession of sins. Pray for other's needs. Ask for

your needs according to God's will, in faith, and in His name.

January 10

For it is by grace you have been saved, through faith-
and this not from yourselves, it is the gift of God.

Ephesians 2:8

Even our faith is not of ourselves. It is a gift from God, by His grace.
Our salvation is because of Jesus. Remember to be thankful to Jesus
for paying our debt in full.

January 11

But the fruit of the Spirit is love, joy, peace, patience, kindness, goodness, faithfulness, gentleness, self-control; against such things there is no law.

Galatians 5:22-23

When we walk with the Spirit, these attributes grow everyday and become active in our lives. There is no law against any of these things. They will produce much fruit in our lives. Be filled with the Holy Spirit of God.

January 12

Therefore, if anyone is in Christ, he is a new creation:

The old has gone, the new has come.

2 Corinthians 5:17

When we come into vital union with Christ, we are made new. We are no longer just living to please the flesh. We are now living for eternity and not just temporal things. Christ lives within us.

January 13

Jesus Christ is the same yesterday, today, and forever.

Hebrews 13:8

He never changes. God intentionally sent Him and every moment of His life as the foundation of our world. Jesus will always remain the same because He is the beginning and the end.

January 14

Finally, brothers, whatever is true, whatever is noble, whatever is right, whatever is pure, whatever is lovely, whatever is admirable - If anything is excellent or praiseworthy - Think about such things.

Philippians 4:8

It is our responsibility as Christians to bring the Light of Jesus into this world. Be POSITIVE, encourage others, give hope, and live in harmony with God's divine standard of holiness. For these things are pleasing to the Lord.

January 15

And we know that all things work together for good to those who are called according to His purpose.

Romans 8:28

The ministry that God will bless you in is the one that He called you to do. It's not the CALLING OF your own choosing, but the one that He has revealed to you through prayer, for His purpose.

January 16

For the Load is good: His mercy is everlasting: And

His truth endureth to all generations.

Psalm 100:5

God is the source of goodness. His love never dies. His sacrifice

redeemed sinners and will carry on for every generation. The Bible will

always remain God's truth.

January 17

Mercy, unto you, and peace and love, be multiplied.

Jude 1:2

Believers who seek God's mercy, receive peace and love. When we

give grace to others, the peace and love in our lives is multiplied.

Forgiveness allows us to receive in abundance.

January 18

For I know the plans I have for you, declares the Lord,

plans to prosper you and not harm you, plans to give

you hope and a future.

Jeremiah 29:11

God's intentions are to bring you blessings. With true repentance,

there will be full restoration. At every crossroad He is with you.

Through every painful moment, and every victory, your relationship with

Him grows stronger. God will provide. His plans are always for your

good. He loves you!

January 19

Rivers of living water will flow from His heart

John 7:38

The Spirit will be given to anyone who believes in Him. Jesus is the "Living Water." Allow His love to flow through you like a river.

January 20

Even more blessed are all who hear the word of God

and pie it into practice.

Luke 11:28

Mary was blessed among women for her obedience to God. Equally,

we are as blessed when we listen and obey the word of God, through

our actions.

January 21

Go into all the world and preach the good news to everyone.

Mark 16:15

This is the great commission. We as Christians are called to spread the good news of Jesus Christ to all who will listen. This is as valid to us today as it was to His disciples.

January 22

We are all saved the same way, by the undeserved

grace of the Lord Jesus.

Acts 15:11

It is by His pure grace and love, in dying for us, that we are all equally

saved. No one person is more deserving than the other for this. All the

glory belongs to God.

January 23

He who calls you is faithful.

1 Thessalonians 5:24

God is the truth. He cannot and will not lie. He is faithful and will fulfill

every promise that He makes. We are chosen by Him, for Him.

January 24

As long as I am in the world, I am the light of the world.

John 9:5

Jesus is the light. He who follows Him shall not live in

DARKNESS BUT shall carry the light of life. In this light, we

must complete what God called us to do, while we are here on earth.

January 25

For where your treasure is, there will be your heart also.

Luke 12:34

Where you put your money, reveals the priorities of your heart. Jesus does not promise us riches if we follow Him. Our treasures come from the way we use our hearts and that is something that can never be stolen.

January 26

I am making everything new.

Revelations 21:5

"Write this down for these words are faithful and true" This does not happen at a specific time. This is done daily through the work of the Spirit. Its a renewal of your state of being. A renewal of your heart.

January 27

Come close to God and He will come close to you.

James 4:8

This is about pursuing an intimate relationship with God. Salvation is not just about submitting to God, it's about your communion with God. The closer you are to knowing Him, the closer you will feel Him with you.

January 28

This hope is a strong and trustworthy anchor for our

souls.

Hebrews 6:19

This is a message of reassurance. A message that tells us we can trust

in God's promises to us, deep in our souls. It's the same way as we trust

an anchor to hold its ship from being swept away. We are safe in His

love.

January 29

For to me, living means opportunities for Christ, and dying-well, that's better yet.

Philippians 1:21

When we make the material things the source of our happiness that is a recipe for disaster. When we choose God to be our source for all things then we are sure to have an abundance of all we need.

January 30

For those who exalt themselves will be humbled, and those who humble themselves will be exalted.

Luke 14:11

When we live in humility and seek God's approval rather than man's, we are using His wisdom and honoring Him. A humble way of life leads to more happiness and less unnecessary pain. Humility is a precious thing to God.

January 31

Heaven and earth will disappear, but my words will

never disappear.

Matthew 24:35

Our human understanding of heaven and earth may change or fade but

the Spiritual Truth and Christ never changes. No matter how finial it

may seem, God's love is never ending.

February

February 1

If God is for us who can ever be against us?

Romans 8:21

God is always there to fight for us. He can even help us live peacefully

with our enemies. Those who come against us, come against God

himself.

February 2

Your roots will grow down into God's love and keep

you strong.

Ephesians 3:17

The result of allowing the Holy Spirit to fill our hearts with love, is a

love that is rooted and grounded and able to grow. When we allow

Christ to live in our hearts, our foundation is strong, and He can love

others through us.

February 3

God is love!

1 John 4:16

We have the love of God filling us UP. THIS is not just for now but forever. There is an incredible peace in knowing that no matter what, even if our own families turn against us, that God is always there giving us His unending love.

February 4

No servant can serve two masters; for either he will hate the one and love the other or else he will be devoted to one and despise the other. You cannot serve God and wealth.

Luke 16:13

Money may serve you at times but it is not your master. We must put our trust in God above anything else. An accumulation of wealth is no substitute for our faith in God. God will supply all of our needs above any riches.

February 5

Look I am coming soon, blessed are those who obey the words of prophecy written in this book.

Revelations 22:7

This signifies and assures that the Lord will certainly come. He will give eternal life to those who live by and speak the truth of the Bible and His Word. Happy are those who obey.

February 6

I am coming soon, bringing with me my reward to pay all the people according to their deeds. I am the Alpha and the Omega, the First and the Last, the Beginning and the End.

Revelations 22:12-13

This is another promise of the return of Jesus. It will be sudden and faithful believers will be rewarded for their good deeds. He is One God in three persons-Father, Son, and Holy Spirit. All the glory belongs to him.

February 7

Christ suffered for our sins once for all time.

1 Peter 3:18

Jesus died on the cross in full payment for our sins. He had no sin himself. Imagine the sacrifice that He and His Father made. We owe him an enormous debt of GRATITUDE.

February 8

My times are in your hands.

Psalm 31:15

There is a special season for everything. Don't rush full speed ahead without checking with God first. Sometimes you will have to wait but God will always direct your next steps at the right time. God's timing is always perfect.

February 9

Jesus quickly spoke to them, He said, "Have courage!

It is I! Don't be afraid!"

Matthew 14:27

Don't just look to all the troubles of this world. Look to Jesus and hear Him saying, "Have courage, don't be afraid." Its easy to be scared or discouraged but we must remember that He is always right beside us, giving us the courage we need.

February 10

I can do all things through Christ because He gives me strength.

Philippians 4:13

Don't worry because your weakness is just a reminder that you need God. Take His hand, trust Him, let Him guide you. He loves to help you and He will lead you every step of the way. God is your strength. He will make you strong.

February 11

God is the one who saves me. I trust Him. I am not

afraid. The Lord gives me strength and makes me sing.

He has saved me.

Isaiah 12:2

God is with YOU. Don't be afraid. Hold onto His right hand and He

will guide you, shelter you, give you strength, and make you sing with joy

again. God will bless you with His joy when you trust Him to help you.

February 12

I pray that you and all God's holy people will have the power to understand the greatness of Christ's love. I pray that you can understand how wide and how long how high and how deep that love is.

Ephesians 3:18

God's love is a promise that will never be broken. No matter what may happen or how bad things may get, His love for you is unshakable and can never be taken away. Try to let go of all your doubts and see yourself as God sees you-beautifully made in His image with love. Your entire life can be built on his love.

February 13

Love is patient and kind. Love is not jealous or boastfu

or proud or rude. It does not demand its own way, it is

not irritable, and it keeps no record of being wronged. It

does not rejoice about injustice but rejoices whenever

the truth wins out. Love never gives up, never loses

faith, is always hopeful, and endures through every

circumstance.

1 Corinthians 13:4-7

This is the ultimate example of God's love for us. It is

UNCONDITIONAL. It's not about the love that you are

receiving, it's about the kind of commitment and the act of love that you

are giving. If we love like God, we will never fail because the greatest of

all the virtues will always remain love.

February 14

Be on guard, stand firm in faith. Be courageous, be strong, and do everything with love.

1 Corinthians 16:13-14

We are One Body in Christ. We are called to be devoted brothers and sisters. We are called to walk together as Christians with bravery and strength. Do not compromise your faith but do what is good, and honest, and pure. We are united together in Him through His love.

February 15

"Come to me, all you who are weary and burdened, and

I will give you rest."

Matthew 11:28

God is with you through all of your troubles. You only need to go to

Him, talk to Him, and tell Him all of your worries. He will give you the

rest that you need and will release your pain and bring peace to your

soul.

February 16

Always be joyful. Never stop praying. Be thankful in all your circumstances, for this is God's will for all who belong to Jesus Christ.

1 Thessalonians 5:16-18

With God it is possible to be joyful even when things are going wrong. When you pray, be thankful always, for He has made the ultimate sacrifice for you. Praising Jesus Christ will add blessings and increase joy in your life. It is important to be grateful in the good times and the bad.

February 17

When troubles of any kind come your way, consider it

an opportunity for great joy.

James 1:2

Living with joy is a choice. You may have to make that choice several

times each day, especially when you are struggling with something. It

may seem impossible but God is teaching you that, in looking for joy

through your troubles there is a great blessing.

February 18

Your beauty and love chase after me every day of my life. I'm back home in the house of God for the rest of my life.

Psalm 23:6

Look for signs of God's Presence every day. He shows up in many different ways. Through a verse in the Bible, through a friend, or even in nature, He will show Himself. Ask for eyes to see God's blessings. They are all around you.

February 19

Do not worry about anything. But instead pray and ask God for everything you need. And when you pray, always give thanks.

Philippians 4:6

When you trust in God in the hard times and you pray with a thankful heart, you give Him all the glory. Go to Him, talk to Him, ask for His guidance. He is always doing something really important in your life. It may not always be in your timing, but your patience and faithfulness will be rewarded.

February 20

Oh Lord, you are our Father. We are the clay, you are the potter, we are all the work of your hand.

Isaiah 64:8

Trust that God is always with you. He is your strength. He is the one who holds you, molds you, and shapes who you become. There is nothing about you that He doesn't know. Tell Him everything you need. His love for you never ends and never fails.

February 21

We urge you in the name of the Lord Jesus, to live in a way that pleases God.

1 Thessalonians 4:1

Seek to please God, the One who knows everything about you. This will change the way you think and live. Your choices matter. No matter how big or small, they must be made with the heart of God in mind.

February 22

Keep your roots deep in Him and have your lives built on Him. Be strong in the faith, just as you were taught. And always be thankful.

Colossians 2:7

The relationship you have with God is the most important relationship. He lives in you and you live in Him. This is the foundation in your life in which you build upon. The more thankful you are, the stronger your house will be. Your life will be filled with joy and blessings.

February 23

The Lord gives strength to His people; the Lord blesses His people with peace.

Psalm 29:11

Learn to see God with the eyes of your heart because He is truly there. We may not be able to see, hear, and touch Him, but His presence is very real. Your prayers to Him make a difference. Trust that He hears you. Breathe in His peace and He will give you rest.

February 24

You will receive your salvation with joy. You will take it as you would draw water from a well.

Isaiah 12:3

The well is deeper than you could ever imagine and it is filled with God's blessings. It represents our salvation. Nothing is of greater value than what He has done for us. His love for us is beyond measure.

February 25

These troubles come to prove that your faith is pure.

This purity of faith is worth more than gold.

1 Peter 1:7

God will use your troubles to make your faith purer. Stay close to Him and He will support you. The closer you are, the easier it will be to face any trials in the future. Don't give up! There is no limit as to how much God can do for you.

February 26

You have shown me the way of life, and you will fill me

with the joy of your presence.

Acts 2:28

Keep your eyes fixed on Jesus and He will show you the world the way

He sees it. Fill your heart with His word and it will light the way to your

path. Seek Him every day and your life will be filled with the joy of His

presence.

March

March 1

Let them praise the Lord for His great love and for the wonderful things He has done for them. Let them offer sacrifices of thanksgiving and sing joyfully about His glorious acts.

Psalm 107:21-22

A grateful heart will only make the joy in your life grow more. Sing to the Lord with a joyful heart and give Him thanks and praise. No matter what is happening in your life, you can still be joyful.

March 2

We capture every thought and make it give up and obey

Christ

2 Corinthians 10:5

Let the light of God's presence enter your mind and destroy all the lies

of the enemy. The more you focus on Him and His word, the easier it

will be to break free from damaging thoughts. Find joy in His truth.

March 3

So be humbled under God's powerful hand. Then He will lift you up when the right time comes. Give all your worries to Him because He cares for you.

1 Peter 5:6-7

Every time you give your worries to God, you are taking your thoughts off your problems, and thinking about Him instead. Be careful what you think about. Humble yourself and put it all in His hands. He is there to protect you always.

March 4

Where God's love is, there is no fear, because God's perfect love takes away fear. It is punishment that makes a person fear. So love is not made perfect in the person who is afraid.

1 John 4:18

Not even your worst mistake can separate you from God's love. When you are faced with a choice, don't let worry or fear cloud your judgement. He will guide you as you think things through with Him. Pray for His will to be done and all will work out as it should.

March 5

Be joyful because you have hope. Be patient when troubles come. Pray at all times.

Romans 12:12

Patience is part of the fruit of the Spirit. Love is patient. When you're having trouble being patient ask the Holy Spirit to help you be more understanding and help you to love others with His patient love. Love others as He loves you.

March 6

Let the peace of Christ rule your hearts, since as members of one body you were called to peace. And be thankful.

Colossians 3:15

Invite the Holy Spirit to fill you with His Peace and enjoy being in His PRESENCE. As you are spending this quiet time with Him, be thankful for the many blessings He has given to you. His peace and love are always available to you.

March 7

You made man a little lower than the angels. And you

crowned him with glory and honor.

Psalm 8:5

God created you perfectly in His own image. Every moment of your

life is made to be meaningful and important. Give Him the glory so that

you can be a reflection of His Glory out in the world. Show His Light

through you and help others come to know Him.

March 8

He is the God of all comfort. He comforts us every time we have trouble, so that we can comfort others when they have trouble. We can comfort them with the same comfort that God gives us.

2 Corinthians 1:3-4

Your pain has a purpose. God is with you always to comfort you through it. Your suffering can make you stronger and prepare you to help others who are struggling. Do not miss the blessings inside of your pain and use them for His purpose. Your understanding will help touch others lives and Peace will grow inside of you and bless you.

March 9

It is a rich land flowing with milk and honey.

Numbers 14:8

God is very generous with us. He supplies us with everything we need.

He is our protector. When we follow Him and are obedient to Him, the

blessings in our lives will be overflowing. All of our needs are met

through our trust in Him and His Love for us.

March 10

God has been very gracious to me. I have more than

enough.

Genesis 33:11

It is important to be grateful for all of the things that God has already

blessed us with. When we see our lives as already being full and see

everything that we already have as more than enough, God is sure to

multiply those blessings.

March 11

True wisdom and power are found in God.

Job 12:13

God is the one who makes it possible to understand. His wisdom never changes. It always remains the same. It is His strength that makes it possible for us to do all things. God is the source of all wisdom and strength.

March 12

Now go. I will be with you as you speak, and I will instruct you what to say.

Exodus 4:12

God will empower you when you allow Him to speak through you. All you need to do is have a willing heart and trust that God will provide you with what you need. The training comes through Him, His word, and what He is asking you to do.

March 13

You saw how the Lord your God cared for you all along the way, just as a father cares for his child.

Deuteronomy 1:31

God is our Father and we are His children. He cares for us and provides for us in every single way. He leads our steps. He provides food, clothing, and protection. He gives us all the love we need. Be grateful, for His Love for us is unconditional and it never ends.

March 14

May the Lord, under whose wings you have come to take refuge, reward you fully for what you have done.

Ruth 2:12

Like a bird protects its young, so does the Lord protect you. You have shelter in Him. Those who go to Him to seek His protection will see all the blessings to follow. Trust in the Lord and you shall prosper.

March 15

The Lord looks at the heart.

1 Samuel 16:7

Your outward appearance does not determine your worth according to the Lord. He looks to see the kind of heart you have. Who you are on the inside and how you choose to live your life in Him, gives Him great joy.

March 16

I trust in your love. My heart is happy because you

saved me.

Psalm 13:5

God is in control. His ways are higher than your ways. You may not

understand all that He does, but it is a reminder to talk to Him. He is

your savior. Trust that His love will never fail you.

March 17

God has made everything beautiful for its own time. He has planted eternity in the human heart.

Ecclesiastes 3:11

God has made a season foe everything in our lives. It is up to us to decide how we behave in each of those seasons. Be grateful, enjoy the fruits of your labor, and be joyful because each moment or blessing He puts before us is a gift.

March 18

You must always act in fear of the Lord, with faithfulness and an undivided heart.

2 Chronicles 19:9

We must live under the commandments of the Lord and do what's right. Encourage others to live according to His ways and He shall take notice. Take courage in Him to fulfill His decrees.

March 19

And He will be called Wonderful Counselor, Mighty God, Everlasting Father, Prince of Peace.

Isaiah 9:6

A child was born to the Virgin Mary, the Son of God. He is our savior. His power is unlimited. He brings Peace among the nations of our world. He is the Messiah and the Father to His people for all eternity.

March 20

Obey me and I will be your God, and you will be my

people. Do everything as I say, and all will be well.

Jeremiah 7:23

Your obedience towards God has a direct effect on the direction your

life will take. When you obey and follow what He is asking you to do,

the outcome will be joyful. With disobedience there is always a price to

pay.

March 21

Pour out your hearts like water to the Lord.

Lamentations 2:19

Lift up your hands in prayer, cry aloud, let your tears fall, and hold nothing back. Bring your every worry to the Lord. He is listening to every word you say. Depend on Him to take care of all of you and all of your burdens. He is waiting for you to go to Him.

March 22

There will be showers of blessings.

Ezekiel 34:26

All gifts come from God. When the flowers need rain, He makes it rain.

Everything works in His perfect timing. Trust that when the time is

right God will provide the blessing that you need.

March 23

The Lord has declared today that you are His people, His own special treasure, just as He promised, and that you must obey all His commandments.

Deuteronomy 26:18

There is no one the Lord loves more than His people. We are His and He is ours. He is our Father, and as His children we must obey His commandments, His decrees, and His regulations. As we do this we shall receive His praise, His honor, and His promises.

March 24

I am always with you; you hold me by my right hand. You guide me with your counsel, and afterward you will take me into glory.

Psalm 73:23-24

God is always with you, holding you by His right hand, showing you the best way to go. He is always doing something new in your life. So don't turn away from the new. Look for Him, ask Him to help you see what He sees, and let Him guide you to His perfect plan for you.

March 25

"Come now, let's settle this." says the Lord. "Though

your sins are like scarlet, I will make them white as snow."

Isaiah 1:18

Even though our sins can be very bad, God is able to cleanse them and

make you clean again. We only need to choose repentance and

obedience in order to receive this gift from Him. He is our salvation.

March 26

I will protect you and your reward will be great.

Genesis 15:1

Christ is your spiritual shield against all things evil, including enemies, sin and Satan. He is your protector. Your faith is your weapon. He who believes in Him shall undoubtably prosper. He will encourage you and cast out your fears.

March 27

Give the following instructions to the entire community. You must be Holy because I the Lord your God am Holy.

Leviticus 19:2

We must try to live our lives Holy, without sin. Walk in holiness because God is Holy and He wants us to try to be more like Him. No one is perfect or without sin except Jesus but He asks us to try our best to emulate Him.

March 28

Fear of the Lord is the foundation of wisdom.

Knowledge of the Holy One results in good

judgement.

Proverbs 9:10

When we fear the Lord, obey Him, and do not rebel against Him, we

set ourselves up to live in His ways. Learning His ways creates the

knowledge we need to make good decisions in our lives. Knowing Him

KEEPS US on the right path, His path, and using good judgement.

March 29

The Sovereign Lord is my strength. He makes me as sure footed as a deer, able to tread upon the heights.

Habakkuk 3:19

Your faith in the Lord will help you to endure the hardships you will undoubtably face. Stand firm in your faith and He will provide you with the strength you need to overcome whatever you are facing. Your security and hope come directly from the Lord Himself.

March 30

I have given rest to the weary and joy to the sorrowing.

Jeremiah 31:25

God will wipe away all your tears of sorrow. He will give you joy and rest and provide you with everything you need abundantly. God is who He says He is. Trust in Him and He will provide.

March 31

Look up to Heaven, His rule is everlasting and His Kingdom eternal.

Daniel 4:34

When we worship and praise our One True God, we are giving Him the glory. When our judgement day comes, we need to repent and ask for His forgiveness, so He can restore us. God's grace allows us to spend an eternity with Him in the Kingdom of Heaven.

April

April 1

Who knows if perhaps you were made queen for just

such a time as this?

Esther 4:14

~ Sometimes God will put a person in a particular place or into a set of

circumstances in order to carry out a specific task. God will use us to

fulfill His perfect plan.

April 2

Don't be afraid of the enemy. Remember the Lord who

is great and glorious.

Nehemiah 4:14

The only power that the enemy has over us is the power that we allow

him to have. Don't be fooled by his lies. God is for us. He is our

protector.

April 3

You are the giver of life. Your light lets us enjoy life.

Psalm 36: 9

You are His child bought with His blood. Look to Jesus, follow Him,
and know He has provided you with so many gifts. Sing His
PRAISES AND go to Him without fear because you are His joy
and you are the one He loves.

April 4

So now I am giving you a new commandment; Love each other. Just as I have loved you, you should love each other. Your love for one another will prove to the world that you are my disciples.

John 13:34-35

God wants us to love as He loves. That doesn't mean to just love the people who are good to us. We must love our enemies as well. As hard as that may be, we need to be the living example of God's love for others to see.

April 5

Yes I am the vine; You are the branches. Those who remain in me, and I in them, will produce much fruit. For apart from me you can do nothing.

John 15:5

We are an extension of God's love. We can try and do things on our own but we will come up short of the abundance God has planned for us if we don't seek Him in all we do. With God the possibilities are endless.

April 6

"I say this because I know what I am planning for you,"

says the Lord." I have good plans for you, not plans to

hurt you, I will give you hope and a good future.

Jeremiah 29:11

God already knows the outcome for you. He has good plans for you

and will present you with many opportunities. You only need to listen,

obey, and trust. Once you discover His path, you must work towards

what He is asking you to do because He created you for a very

important reason.

April 7

Be cheerful no matter what; pray all the time; thank God no matter what happens.

1 Thessalonians 5: 16-18

It is important to have an attitude of gratitude. When we are too busy, sometimes it is easy to lose sight of what is really important. When we take time to thank God no matter what is happening in our lives it brings Him great joy.

April 8

The Lord is my rock and my fortress and my deliverer;

the God of my strength, in whom I will trust.

2 Samuel 22:2-3

Although we may face struggles and disappointments we must always

remember that we never do it alone. God is always there right beside us

to help us along the way. We only need to look up and have faith that

His infinite love for us helps us to meet our challenges.

April 9

He comforts us in all our affliction, so that we may be
able to comfort those who are in any kind of affliction,
through the comfort we ourselves receive from God.

2 Corinthians 1:4

We can begin to soften our own troubles when we recognize the needs
of others. Sometimes we experience difficult times in order to help
someone else get through the very same thing. BE SURE to
encourage, instill hope and help others.

April 10

Indeed we count them blessed who endure.

James 5:11

Sometimes obstacles can come against us but if we remain persistent

we can change the outcome of what we are facing. God wants us to be

as persistent in pursuing Him as we are in pursuing our dreams.

April 11

I will bless them and the places surrounding my hill. I will send down showers in season; there will be showers of blessing.

Ezekiel 34:26

It is important to give thanks to the biggest giver of all. All of our blessings are because of God. Take the time each day to say thank you for the many things He has blessed you with. When you share those blessings with others He will be sure to multiply them.

April 12

A cheerful disposition is good for your health; gloom

and doom leave you bone-tired.

Proverbs 17:22

God has given us the gift of laughter for a very good reason. Taking

the time out to be playful and laugh is a recipe for a healthy life. God

wants us to be happy and enjoy ourselves. It will keep us young at heart.

April 13

Man does not see what the Lord sees, for man sees
what is visible, but the lord sees the heart.

1 Samuel 16:7

Outward appearances are of no importance to God. He sees our
hearts and understands us by how we use them. He sees us for who we
really are on the inside. Focus on becoming the best version of yourself
based on what God sees.

April 14

For we are God's workmanship, created in Jesus Christ to do good works, which God prepared in advance for us to do.

Ephesians 2:10

God has created us each uniquely for a specific purpose. We need to acknowledge the opportunities that He has put into our lives and put them to good use. He has prepared a specific path for us and it's up to us to follow it.

April 15

Discipline yourself for the purpose of godliness.

1 Timothy 4:7

If you want to maximize what God has given to you then you need to be self disciplined. God will give you the gifts but you will need to work at them to get the most out of them. With discipline you will get to where you want to be.

April 16

The Lord bless you and keep you: The Lord make His face shine upon you and be gracious to you.

Numbers 6:24-25

A grateful heart is even more blessed than and ungrateful heart. Make sure to take the time every day for all the blessings He has bestowed upon you. Great joy comes from focusing on your blessings instead of your problems.

April 17

God is pleased with you when, for the sake of your conscience, you patiently endure unfair treatment.

1 Peter 2:19

There is a still quiet voice that speaks to your heart that God has instilled. That inner voice is our conscience and it tells us right from wrong. Remember to always listen to that voice or there may be consequences to face.

April 18

Commit to the Lord whatever you do, and your plans

will succeed.

Proverbs 16:3

If you believe in yourself and believe that with God anything can

happen, then you will succeed. Don't worry about what anybody else

says. Focus on who your God is and with time and effort anything is

possible.

April 19

We're not giving up. How could we! Even though on the outside it often looks like things are falling apart on us, on the inside, where God is making new life, not a day goes by without His unfolding grace.

2 Corinthians 4:16

Things can feel like they are completely spiraling out of control sometimes. In those times, remember that God is with you and He is doing something new in your life. Despite how difficult things may be He is always there loving you and keeping His promises to you.

April 24

Above all these things put on charity, which is the bond of perfectness.

Colossians 3:14

It is one of the commandments that we love thy neighbor. That means God wants us to take the time out of our days to help each other. It is more important than most people make the time for. When we make this a priority in our lives God makes the things we need His priority.

April 25

If you make a promise to God, don't be slow to keep it. God is not happy with fools, so give God what you promised.

Ecclesiastes 5:4

Procrastination avoids what needs to be done and only causes more stress on oneself. When we make a habit of doing what is necessary right away we avoid the unnecessary troubles that procrastination may cause. God will reward those who will do it now.

April 26

God has no use for prayers of the people who don't

listen to Him.

Proverbs 28:9

Are you taking time out each day to really hear what the Lord is asking

of you? He will not come to you with bells and WHISTLES. His

voice is still and quiet. So it is in those still and quiet moments that you

take the time to spend with Him so that you truly hear what He is

asking you to do.

April 27

Fill us with your love every morning. Then we will sing

and rejoice all our lives.

Psalm 90:14

Sometimes we try to fill our lives up with all the human things of the

world. The truth is that nothing can truly fill us up like our Lord.

Spending time with Him each day will fill your life with joy above all

things. There may still be troubles but God's perfect love will always

see you through them.

April 28

Remember: A stingy planter gets a stingy crop; a lavish planter gets a lavish crop.

2 Corinthians 9:6

God has freely given us so many gifts. We can repay Him by giving to others as freely as He has given to us. It doesn't just have to be in the form of money but our time and our love are of equal importance. Show your great love for God with your generosity.

April 29

Be angry, and sin not: let not the sun go down upon

your wrath.

Ephesians 4:26

In this world there is no doubt that the innocent will be wronged. We

need to go to God with these wrongdoings in prayer and seek His

guidance. We are to let go of these things and leave them for God to

handle. He will make wrong things right.

April 30

"Who of you by being worried can add a single hour to his life?"

Matthew 6:27

God is in control! He will always set our paths straight. Not one single moment of worry will change the outcome of your circumstances. So just trust in Him and He will provide you with everything you need.

May

May 1

If you live according to the sinful nature, you will die; but
if by the Spirit you put to death the misdeeds of the
body, and you will live.

Romans 8:13

Focusing on only your worldly needs will lead to a path of emptiness.
When you live your life through Christ and His Spirit, the blessings
will come in abundance. An obedient life is an abundant life.

May 2

I have learned in whatever state I am, to be content.

Philippians 4:11

God knows everything that is happening in our lives. It is important to

trust Him with all of our needs. Be grateful for the things He has

already provided and grateful for being where you are right now, and

He will take care of your future.

May 3

God raised him from the dead, freeing him from the

agony of death, because it was impossible for death to

keeps its hold on him.

Acts 2:24

We can share in Jesus' eternal life when we give our lives to Him. God

sacrificed His only son in order to pay for our sins and free us from the

agony of death. Jesus has brought us hope.

May 4

This is the promise that He has promised us–eternal life.

1 John 2:25

Trust in the unfailing promise of eternal life that comes from God. When we receive Jesus in our hearts that love will continue even after death. In eternity we will be reunited with the ones that we loved here on earth.

May 5

Be merciful to those who doubt.

Jude 1:22

When we are having feelings of uncertainty it doesn't help when people

criticize our feelings. Just as we need someone to be encouraging to us

in those times, we need to be as encouraging to others when they are

having doubts.

May 6

He has also set eternity in the hearts of men; yet they cannot fathom what God had done from beginning to end.

Ecclesiastes 3:11

We cannot possibly fathom all the works of our God. Therefore, we should trust that our Father, the Alpha and Omega is in control. We each have a part of Him in our hearts that promises eternity with Him.

May 7

Looking unto Jesus the author and finisher of our faith.

Hebrews 12:2

No matter what trials you may face on this earthly life, the outcome is always going to remain the same when we love Jesus. Even though we may suffer, when we turn to Jesus during THOSE TIMES He offers us His protection and gives us new strength. Our lives begin and end with Him.

May 8

His works are perfect, and all His ways are just. A faithful God who does no wrong, upright and just is he.

Deuteronomy 32:4

God is always faithful, perfect, and just. His ways are not our ways but when we follow Him He will make sure to lead us all the way to the Promised Land to Him. Trust in Him always.

May 9

How blessed are those whose way is blameless, who

walk in the law of the Lord.

Psalm 119:1

Living an obedient life is one that pleases the Lord. An obedient life is

a blessed life. Do not ignore His commands and He will provide you

with a life filled with joy.

May 10

The rod of correction imparts wisdom, but a child left to

himself disgraces his mother.

Proverbs 29:15

Just as God restrains us from wrongdoing, we need to do the same for

our children. In doing so we are giving them the wisdom to chose right

from wrong. Helping them to modify their behavior will teach them how

to love better.

May 11

You ought to forgive and comfort him, so that he will

not be overwhelmed by excessive sorrow.

2 Corinthians 2:7

When you know someone who is struggling with their sins and truly

sorry for them, then you should try to bring them comfort just as you

would want for yourself. You can be a great blessing to someone else

who is hurting.

May 12

Each one of you also must love his wife as he loves

himself, and the wife must respect her husband.

Ephesians 5:33

God created marriage as reflection of His own love for us. For us to

have a healthy relationship it must be filled with love and respect for one

another. Both husband wife have to be willing to give and receive.

Love, honor, and respect are a recipe for a happy home.

May 13

"Honor your father and your mother, that your days

may be long upon the land."

Exodus 20:12

This is one of the commandments that we must follow. When we give

our parents respect, God reserves many blessings for us. Showing our

parents respect not only strengthens our relationship with them but

also with God.

May 14

You came near when I called you, and you said, "Do not fear."

Lamentations 3:57

God is not the creator of fear. The enemy tries to attack us with fear to keep us from our destination. Our freedom is in our Redeemer who saves us from every harm. Be not afraid for He is always with us.

May 15

"If you forgive others for their transgressions, your heavenly Father will also forgive you."

Matthew 6:14

Just as our Father forgives us, He commands us to forgive others for their sins. Even though it may be difficult sometimes to forgive we must do it as many times as we need to in order to live the best life that God has planned for us.

May 16

"It is more blessed to give than receive"

Acts 20:35

When we are giving to others we are sharing the same love that God has for us. Don't let greed motivate you but instead give more of what you have to others and great blessing will fill up your life.

May 17

How great is the love the Father has lavished on us, that we should be called children of God! And that is what we are!

1 John 3:1

We are all God's children and when we obey Him as His children, there is nothing that He can't do in our lives. He is just waiting for us to go to Him and ask for His help. WE are so blessed to be loved so much by our Father.

May 18

Nothing in all creation is hidden from God's sight.

Hebrews 4:13

God knows everything that is happening in our lives. He sees all the good and all the troubles that we face. He uses every aspect of our lives to our benefit and will always provide us with the support we need.

May 19

Mercy triumphs over judgement!

James 2:13

We are meant to show the same compassion towards others as God shows us. We must stand firm in our good works and not pass judgment on other people. May we show the same mercy that God has show us.

May 20

He saved us, not because of righteous things we had done, but because of His mercy. He saved us through the washing of rebirth and renewal by the Holy Spirit.

Titus 3:5

With God's mercy and the sacrifice of His only Son, we have been saved. Without God there is no way this could have happened. Give thanks for we are renewed by the Father, Son and Holy Spirit.

May 21

"Then I will make up to you for the years that the

swarming locust has eaten."

Joel 2:25

Though we may endure hardships in our lives, God makes a promise to

restore all that has been lost to those who are faithful. We can trust

that God is able to turn any situation around. Faith will help return

prosperity to those who love Him.

May 22

"I will turn their mourning into gladness; I will give them comfort and joy instead of sorrow."

Jeremiah 31:13

Your sorrow can be turned into joy. Seek the Lord boldly and ask for His help. He is capable of turning every bit of your pain into something positive. When we focus on Him He gives us the strength we need to overcome anything.

May 23

Do you not know that you are the temple of God and that the Spirit of God dwells in you?

1 Corinthians 3:16

Devote your life to the Lord for He lives within you. He is never far because He fills you up with the Holy Spirit. You have the power to live a holy life and find your strength in Him.

May 24

Live a life of love, just as Christ loved us and gave himself up for us as a fragrant offering and sacrifice to God.

Ephesians 5:2

Jesus made the ultimate sacrifice for us. That's the kind of love He has for us. We are not meant to just receive this kind of love but we are to give it to others and make sacrifices to those who need help to understand His love better.

May 25

In Him was life, and that life was the light of men.

John 1:4

When we are following Jesus we are living in the Light of Christ. Believers need to make the necessary changes in order to clean out the dark places in their lives. Our light will shine and help draw others closer to Christ.

May 26

"All these blessings shall come upon you and overtake you, cause you obey the voice of the Lord your God."

Deuteronomy 28:2

It's not just when we obey God then the very next moment something good happens for us. Sometimes the blessings takes longer than we think they should. It's consistently obeying and doing the work He has called us to do then God will fulfill His promises to us.

May 27

"Therefore I tell you, whatever you ask for in prayer, believe that you have received it, and it will be yours."

Mark 11:24

Are we asking for things according to God's will? Is IT SOMETHING self indulgent or will it help others? Is what you are asking for glorifying God in any way? These are the things we should consider in our prayers. God answers our prayers when we are in a position to receive.

May 28

The Lord is my Shepard I shall not want.

Psalm 23:1

When we look to our leader, our Shepherd there is nothing that we cannot overcome. Those who follow Jesus will be provided for abundantly. He will guide you through every step of your life and fill you with His Spirit.

May 29

We live by faith, not by sight.

2 Corinthians 5:7

God is capable of giving us eyes to see things as He sees them. When we chose to see things in faith and not just what our physical eyes can see, we are able to make better decisions on the path that God is leading us to.

June 2

"In your unfailing love you will lead the people you have redeemed. In your strength you will guide them to your holy dwelling."

Exodus 15:13

No matter how far off course you may get, God is always there right beside you, loving you and ready to make your crooked path straight. Seek Him in all you do and He will guide you and give you strength.

June 3

"And if he sins against you seven times in a day, and seven times in a day returns to you, saying, 'I repent,' you shall forgive him."

Luke 17:4

Are we quick to forgive others when they offend us? God wants us to give the same kind of forgiveness that he gives us. When we show that kind of compassion towards others, God blesses us.

June 4

Jesus gave himself for us to redeem us from all wickedness and to purify for himself a people that are his very own, eager to do what is good.

Titus 2:14

People can change but God is capable making the most amazing changes in the most sinful people. Jesus payed for our sins so we are all able to be redeemed. Turn to God and He will lead us to holiness.

June 5

All Scripture is useful for training in righteousness, so that the man of God may be thoroughly equipped for every good work.

2 Timothy 3:16-17

The Bible is your guide. God has prepared all of these scriptures that tells us all we need to know. Believers will know how to put into action what He has laid out for us. Love like Him, act like Him, live like Him.

June 6

You were called to be free. But do not use your freedom to indulge the sinful nature; rather, serve one another in love.

Galatians 5:13

God freed us from our sin so that we can share His love with others. Rather than indulging in the sinful ways of the world, we should use all God has provided to help serve others.

June 7

Try to excel in gifts that build up the church.

1 Corinthians 14:12

When God gave you that beautiful spiritual gift it wasn't just so you could serve yourself. How are you using your gift to serve others? Are you drawing people closer with His word? We need to help support others with our gifts and draw new believers to Him.

June 8

Only be strong and very courageous, that you may observe to do according to all the law which Moses My servant commanded you; do not turn from it to the right hand to the left, that you may prosper wherever you go.

Joshua 1:7

Being obedient to God's commandments can bring you great prosperity. Things may not always happen in your timing but God is always faithful to His promises.

June 9

Because He Himself suffered when He was tempted,

He is able to help those who are being tempted.

Hebrews 2:18

Satan will try everything he can to temp us into sinful ways. Because

Jesus was tempted himself, He knows just what we feel when we are

trying to resist. Jesus never gave into the temptations that were put in

front of Him. Therefore, we can look to Him to help us face anything

we are up against.

June 10

Because of the Lord's great love we are not consumed,

for His compassions never fail.

Lamentations 3:22

The compassion that God has for us is endless. When we have hope in our hearts God can strengthen us with His deep love. No matter what trials we may face God is there to comfort us and hold us up.

June 11

Love the Lord your God with all you heart and with all your soul and with all your mind.

Matthew 22:37

It doesn't seem possible that we could ever fall short of this considering everything that God has done for us. But we are human and sometimes we fall short. Make it a priority everyday to follow this commandment and watch how complete your life will become.

June 12

Dear friends, let us love one another, for love comes from God. Everyone who loves has been born of God and knows God.

1 John 4:7

Love isn't something we just feel but its an action; a clear decision to lead someone to follow Christ. It's the constant efforts that we make to show others we care. There is no more perfect love than God's love for us. Let's try to express our love a little more like Him.

June 13

Whatever you do, work at it with all your heart, as working for the Lord not for man.

Colossians 3:23

The only one who you are truly accountable to is Jesus. So whatever you do in your life do it to please Him and not try to please man. We have one judge and jury and it is not anyone here on earth. Make sure to do everything with love.

June 14

Make it your ambition to lead a quiet life, to mind your own business and to work with your hands.

1 Thessalonians 4:11

We each have something to contribute. No matter what you choose for a career, know that God has created you perfectly and has given you everything you need to accomplish it. You can still be a leader while remaining quiet and humble.

June 15

God made everything with a place and purpose.

Proverbs 16:4

You get one life to live and it's up to you to make the most of it. God created each of us for a very specific purpose. Take the time to do something that will bless someone else. Do something that will glorify God.

June 16

In quietness and in confidence shall be your strength.

Isaiah 30:15

We need to take quiet times in our days to spend with the Lord. Don't

allow the distractions of the world to separate you from God's peace.

Nothing is more important than our quiet time with God so that we may

hear His directions. His eternal love is our strength.

June 17

Prove yourself doers of the word, and not merely

hearers.

James 1:22

The enemy will use anything he can to try to pressure you into sinning.

Be mindful of the positions you put yourself in, choose carefully what

you watch on T.V., and who you surround yourself with. Making these

choices will make it easier to follow God's word.

June 18

The Lord has sought for Himself a man after His own
heart.

1 Samuel 13:14

God loves the underdog. He wants to use the unlikely person to show
who He really is. He is not seeking someone with all the wealth and
talents and outward appearances. He will find the one who knows His
heart and use them for His good.

June 19

He who is faithful in a very little thing is faithful also in much.

Luke 16:10

If you want God to do very big things in your life then you will have to show Him that you are faithful when only small things are happening. God will only bless you with more when you are grateful for what you already have.

June 20

If it is possible, as much as depends on you, live

peaceably with all men.

Romans 12:18

When God asks us to live peaceably He's not saying only with people

who are good to us. He does not want us to seek revenge on those who

have wronged us. Live in peace and leave the rest to Him.

June 21

What does the Lord require of you but to do justice, to love kindness, and to walk humbly with your God?

Micah 6:8

This is about grace. Grace is a demonstration of unconditional love. Love that is not earned, not deserved, and not repayable. We could never repay God for the grace He has given us, but He wants us to show this kind of grace towards others.

June 22

He brought me out into a broad place; He delivered me

because He delighted in me.

2 Samuel 22:20

When times are tough we can always count on the Lord to be there by

our side. It brings Him great joy to be there for us. Rely on Him

because He is our security and strength. He delights in us.

June 23

Therefore be imitators of God and walk in love.

Ephesians 5:1-2

We are meant to be in each OTHERS' lives. God brings us together to be a community. We as a community make up the church. It is important for us to come together in Christ and draw each other closer to Him. We need to support and encourage each other.

June 24

He who comes to God must believe that He is and that

He is a rewarder of those who seek Him.

Hebrews 11:6

God wants you to go to Him with everything. He wants you to have full

reliance on Him. Wether it be about your children, or finances, or a

choice you need to make, He wants you to check in with Him first

before moving forward.

June 25

My God shall supply all your needs according to His riches in glory in Christ Jesus.

Philippians 4:19

It is petty much a guarantee that you are going to face some adversity in your life. It is up to you to decide what you are going to do with it. You can either stay in your troubles or you can seek God and find joy again.

June 26

You are Christ's body, and individually members of it.

1 Corinthians 12:27

We are all part of Christ's body but He has made us all uniquely different and for a very specific purpose. Just as the animals and the birds all have a job to do, so do we. Be sure to do what God is calling you to do.

June 27

Applying all diligence, in your faith supply moral excellence.

2 Peter 1:5

Are you living in harmony with what God wants? If you have a heart for God then you will be checking in with Him in all you do.

June 28

The Lord is a refuge for His people and a stronghold.

Joel 3:16

If we take refuge in the Lord we can avoid some the strongholds that

the enemy can have against us. Let God be your stronghold. Let His

ways be your ways.

June 29

It is written that the Christ would suffer and rise again from the dead the third day, and that repentance for forgiveness of sins would be proclaimed in His name.

Luke 24:46-47

This was Jesus' fulfillment of what His Father's plan was for Him. Even though He painfully suffered Jesus was determined to follow through with what He was called to do. There was nothing helpless about Jesus. He is our helper, our savior, and He paid for our sins.

June 30

God demonstrates His own love toward us, in that

while we were yet sinners, Christ died for us.

Romans 5:8

Jesus secured our eternal destiny with two pivotal moments in history.

First He died on the cross for us, then three days later He rose from

the dead. It was tragedy to triumph in a matter of days. How blessed

are we that He loves us this much!

July

July 1

Humble yourselves in the presence of the Lord, and

He will exalt you.

James 4:10

God loves a humble person. He wants us to show Him that we need Him. We can have some authority or abundance in our lives but we need to be aware that none of these things would be possible without God.

July 2

I do not seek My own will, but the will of Him who sent

Me.

John 5:30

Even Jesus did everything as God instructed Him to do. He gave up

His own independence to seek the will of His Father. We should be

using Him as an example to follow. He suffered plenty but still showed

obedience.

July 3

Walk in a manner worthy of the God who calls you into His own kingdom and glory.

1 Thessalonians 2:12

If you want to walk with God then you are going to have to make a conscience effort to let go of some of the sinful behaviors and strongholds that are currently in your lives. This is not something that will happen overnight but if you work at it daily you will be one step closer.

July 4

Your light will break out like the dawn, and your recovery will speedily spring forth.

Isaiah 58:8

We all have to process things that are happening in our lives. If things are especially difficult just remember that Jesus is our light and He will always do something new in your life. He will shine His light in your life.

July 5

Everything God does will remain forever; there is nothing to add to it and there is nothing to take from it.

Ecclesiastes 3:14

God is in our lives in everything that we do. That never changes. No matter what we go through, He never leaves us. Seek Him in all that you do because His love for us is everlasting.

July 6

Our citizenship is in heaven, from which also we eagerly

wait for a Savior, the Lord Jesus Christ.

Philippians 3:20

Even though we live here in this world our true citizenship does not

belong here. We are only here for a short time then our true selves

belong to the Kingdom of Heaven. We are meant to do the best we

can to draw others to that community.

July 7

If we have died with Christ, we believe that we shall also

live with Him.

Romans 6:8

There is only one way that we can assure hope after we have passed. If

we are living our lives in faith through Christ then we can have that

assurance. Life with Christ here and in heaven are the epitome of

Hope.

July 8

Christ redeemed us from the curse of the Law, having

become a curse for us.

Galatians 3:13

How blessed are we to have someone love us so much that He actually

died for us? Jesus is our Redeemer. We are free because of Him. Take

the time every day to give Him thanks for that amazing gift.

July 9

I have no greater joy than this, to hear my children

walking in the truth.

3 John 1:4

When we are walking in the word of God we are walking in the truth.

Nothing brings Him greater joy than to see us practicing our walk with

Him. Be a leader and teach others about your God and what it's like

to walk with Him.

July 10

Godliness actually is a means of great gain when accompanied by contentment.

1 Timothy 6:6

If we are living a godly life then the contentment will follow. How are you spending your time and who are you helping? We are not meant to be self indulgent. We are meant to help others then God helps us.

July 11

Walk in a manner worthy of the calling with which you have been called, with all humility and gentleness.

Ephesians 4:1-2

When we release the anger of the wrongdoings that have been done to us then we make more room to fill our lives with joy. Forgive freely and quickly and give those offenses to God. He will take care of the rest.

July 12

Choose life in order that you may live.

Deuteronomy 30:19

God gave us the freedom to make choices. He gave us the opportunity to choose the kind of life we want to live. Really consider what choices you are making and how those choices are affecting your life.

July 13

By this all men will know that you are my disciples, if you

have love for one another.

John 13:35

Our behavior is something that we need to be constantly aware of. If

we are acting in sinful ways on a regular basis, how are we to draw

others closer to Christ? We belong to the Kingdom of Heaven, so

shouldn't we behave that way?

July 14

Wisdom is in the presence of the one who has

understanding.

Proverbs 17:24

Showing a person gratitude will express our appreciation for them. But when we acknowledge the kind of person they are or the things they are going through, it helps them to feel understood. Helping someone to feel understood helps them to affirm who they are.

July 15

He has satisfied the thirsty soul, and the hungry soul

He has filled with what is good.

Psalm 107:9

Christ our Lord is living right inside of you. When we are making the choice to fill our lives with Christ, we shall never be hungry or thirsty again. He provides us with everything we need.

July 16

God is not unjust so as to forget your work and the love which you have shown toward His name.

Hebrews 6:10

The work we do isn't just the job that we go to every day. It's the things that we are doing in between that glorify God and typically earn no reward. Helping a neighbor, paying for someone's groceries, leaving a big tip for a waitress, are all small things we can do that qualify as the work of God.

July 17

Whoever loves the Father loves the child born of Him.

1 John 5:1

We are all God's children and that makes us family. We should be treating each other as such. So when you are feeling intolerant or a lack of understanding towards someone else then you should consider the acceptance that you need yourself and emulate that.

July 18

He will surely be gracious to you at the sound of your

cry; when He hears it, He will answer you.

Isaiah 30:19

Be sure to make your petitions very specific with what you are asking

for from God. He is happy to give us the things we need if it is asked

according to His will. He will qualify you for the very thing you are

asking for if it's in line with His path.

July 19

He is the Lord of lords and the King of kings, and those who are with Him are the called and chosen and faithful.

Revelation 17:14

We only have one God and He is the One who is continuously at work in our lives. He is the only one who knows the prophecy of our lives. Without Him we are nothing. Follow Him and He will make your path straight.

July 20

He makes the nations great, then destroys them; He enlarges the nations, then leads them away.

Job 12:23

God has a very specific plan in place. He knows exactly what is going to happen and when it's going to happen. He is the who, what, when, where, and how of our entire lives. Don't give up. He will make a way.

July 21

Let us not lose heart in doing good, for in due time we will reap if we do not grow weary.

Galatians 6:9

All things are in God's control. We must trust in this wholeheartedly. Even if things are very painful and even if we cannot see the good things He has in store, if we stand firm in our faith and the plans He has for us, blessings are sure to follow.

July 22

Do not tremble or be dismayed, For the Lord your God is with you wherever you go.

Joshua 1:9

God is busy arranging things in your life every single day. In the unexplainable moments, look up and know that it was Him working in your favor. Put the worries behind you because God will never leave you.

July 23

It does not depend on the man who wills or the man who runs, but on God who has mercy.

Romans 9:16

It doesn't matter how hard you may try, if it is not God's will it's not gonna happen. So step aside and let your Father do His work. Go to Him and ask your Father, "What are your plans for me? Where do you want me to go? Who do you need me to help? How can I serve you?"

July 24

To Him be dominion forever and ever.

1 Peter 5:11

God is your ultimate protecter. Even if you have to crawl through the

trenches for a little while, He is right there crawling through those

trenches beside you. There is nothing too big for Him to handle. Trust

in Him. His love never fails.

July 25

Weeping may last for the night, but a shout of joy

comes in the morning.

Psalm 30:5

After your tears have fallen you can be sure that the joy will come

again. Everyone has something in their lives that they are up against

but God hears all of our tears and His promises of hope are

guaranteed to wipe away those tears and bring you joy many more

times.

July 26

I heard the voice of many angels all around the throne saying with a loud voice, "Worthy is the Lamb that was slain to receive power and riches and wisdom and strength and honor and blessing and glory."

Revelations 5:11-12

Imagine the image of the angels surrounding our Lord Jesus and singing His praises. I can't think of anything that would be a more angelic sound than that. Sing out loud. Spread the word. Jesus is the Lamb of God.

July 27

Holy, Holy, Holy is the Lord of hosts.

Isaiah 6:3

"Lord of hosts" What does that mean to you? God cannot be reduced to anything that we can completely comprehend. He will remain a mystery but will always be trustworthy. There is no one more holy than He but holy in Him are we.

July 28

He will exalt over you with joy, He will be quiet in His love.

Zephaniah 3:17

Just because there isn't a firework show on a daily basis doesn't mean that God's love is not as big as that. He may be silent in your life at times but His love is very real and always present. He is there when the day is mundane, He is there for the celebrations, He is there for you always.

July 29

The fruit of the righteous is a tree of life, and he who is

wise wins souls.

Proverbs 11:30

The willingness to learn and remain teachable speaks volumes about a

persons character. At any moment in our lives we could face a situation

that becomes something of great importance. We can then apply what

we learned from those experiences to our future. Don't let a single

moment pass you by without learning something. It may not only help

you some day, it may also help someone else.

July 30

If anyone is in Christ, he is a new creature, the old things passed away; behold, new things have come.

2 Corinthians 5:17

Don't let past pains become a never-ending problem in your life. Hand those misfortunes over to God and don't keep reliving them. He Has something entirely new planned for you and it does not include anything that you have already experienced.

July 31

The battle is the Lord's, and He will give you into our

hands.

1 Samuel 17:47

Give all your fears, your worries, and your doubts over to the Lord.
Those things do not come from Him. He wants us to be filled with Him
and leave everything in His hands. He is our strength.

August

August 1

Even if I am being poured out as a drink offering upon

the sacrifice and service of your faith, I rejoice and

share my joy with you all.

Philippians 2:17

If we are willing to help someone else even in the midst of our own

suffering then we are bringing tremendous joy to God. That is what we

are here for. To help each other not just ourselves.

August 2

Set your mind on the things above, not on the things

that are on earth.

Colossians 3:2

Will you answer God's call? We are all called. Called to rally together

in His honor, Called to add Him to every aspect of your life. Called to

draw others closer to Him. Are you listening?

August 3

Do not be surprised at the fiery ordeal among you,

which comes upon you for your testing.

1 Peter 4:12

When the enemy knows something really good is about to bless your

life, you can be sure that he's gonna come after you with blazing

saddles. There won't be anything he won't try to get you down. Stay

committed to your God! He's has big plans for you!

August 4

Blessed is a man who preservers under trial; for he shall receive the crown of life that the Lord has promised.

James 1:12

Perseverance comes with the full submission to God. How are you facing your trials? Are you trying to do it alone or do it with God? He will pull you through and lead you to all of His PROMISES. Do you believe?

August 5

Make me understand the way of Your precepts, so I will meditate on Your wonders.

Psalm 119:27

How much time are you spending with the Lord? It is even more important than brushing your teeth. You make the effort every day to do that so if spending time with the Lord is even more important, then you should definitely carve out the time daily to make that happen.

Read that Bible!

August 6

Call to me and I will answer you, and I will tell you great

and mighty things, which you do not know.

Jeremiah 33:3

Call to Him. He is there waiting to listen, waiting to help. When you are

at a crossroads and you are unsure of which path to take, call your

Father because He has all the answers. Anytime, day or night, He is

there.

August 7

Dispense true justice and practice kindness and compassion each to his brother.

Zechariah 7:9

True compassion seeks no reward. The act of kindness should be more of a way of life, not something that we receive a monetary gain from. The closer you are to God, the more you will know how to be this way.

August 8

You have granted me life and lovingkindness; and Your

care has preserved my spirit.

Job 10:12

There is only one of you. God created you uniquely for a purpose in His own image. God KNEW EVERYTHING about you while you were being formed in your mothers womb. Every detail about you was on purpose to be used for His glory.

August 9

The Son of Man did not come to be served, but to serve.

Mark 10:45

If God sent His only Son to serve, what do you think he expects of us? He wants His people to have the same giving spirit as His Son. He wants us to serve Him by taking care of His people. How have you been serving God?

August 10

Whatever a man sows, this he will also reap.

Galatians 6:7

This is an important part of Scripture because it clearly says, be careful of your choices because how you choose to act and what you choose to do, will come back to you. Wouldn't you rather have all of God's goodness come back to you?

August 11

Not one of the good promises which the Lord had made to the house of Israel had failed; all came to pass.

Joshua 21:45

God keeps His promises to us. He is faithful. Even though it can sometimes feel like we are on a roller coaster ride in life, He is there at every twist and turn and in the end we will be joyful.

August 12

You shall remember all the way which the Lord your God has led you in the wilderness, that He might humble you, testing you to know what was in your heart, whether you would keep His commands.

Deuteronomy 8:2

God wants us to stand firm in our faith. Therefore He will test our endurance by putting us in uncomfortable situations. Will you choose Him and follow His commands? Will you be obedient to His word?

August 13

You did not choose Me, but I chose you.

Remember who your creator is. He is the reason you are here. We are His children and He is our Father. He wants us to be family. He wants us to come together and unify in His love.

John 15:16

August 14

With humility of mind regard one another as more

important than yourselves.

Philippians 2:3

It's better to be a giver rather than a receiver. Keeping this mentality

omits the tendency to be selfish. When we are encouraging, supporting,

and giving to others, we are honoring God and His ways.

August 15

I hope in You, O Lord; You will answer, O Lord my God.

Psalm 38:15

This is about your commitment to the Lord. How deep is your faith? Put all of your trust in Him. He is the source of our hope. He will answer your prayers when asked according to His will.

August 16

Put on love, which is the perfect bond of unity.

Colossians 3:14

There is no greater bond than the gift of love. Love is not just a verb or a feeling; It's an action. A conscience choice to selflessly treat someone with great importance. To attend to their needs above your own. To give of oneself without expecting return. God loves us this way.

August 17

I have surely seen the affliction of My people...and have

heard their cry ...I know their sorrows.

Exodus 3:7

If you are struggling and find yourself in a situation that seems so

unfair, rest assure that God has seen and heard everything. He has

seen your troubles. He has heard your cry. Trust in Him because He

always has the final say.

August 18

How much better is it to get wisdom than gold. And to get understanding is to be chosen above silver.

Proverbs 16:16

There is nothing wrong with a person who acquires a little bit of wealth. Are you seeking fortune to gain more materials or are you seeking to share it and help others? When your motives are pure in your wealth, then God will bless you with more. When you are satisfied and grateful for what you have already, He blesses you with more.

August 19

The one who does the will of God lives forever.

1 John 2:17

No matter what the circumstances that you are in you always need to remember to check in with God first. When you do this, you can know for certain that you are in line with the will of God. It can range from the smallest to most difficult choices but if it is his will He will make it happen.

August 20

He Himself is our peace.

Ephesians 2:14

Don't let yourself get bogged down by fears and insecurities. Release

all of your worries unto God because He is your one true source of

peace. He will set you free from any of your difficult situations and

relieve you of your burdens.

August 21

The Lord longs to be gracious to you, and therefore

He waits on high to have compassion on you.

Isaiah 30:18

It brings the Lord great joy to give you exactly what you need. He is

happy to provide for you. Give Him thanks every day for all the things

He has done for you because He deserves our appreciation above all

August 22

Blessed be the Lord your God who delights in you...

1 Kings 10:9

"If God is for you who can be against?" He is with us every step of the
way. He is there in our joys and sorrows, in our strengths and
weaknesses. With our faith in Him we can count on Him for anything.

August 23

Let us not become boastful, challenging one another, envying one another.

Galatians 5:26

You will self sabotage by seeking fame in your own name. God is happy to advance you and shine the light on you if you are doing it to glorify Him. Your selflessness and ability to help others rather than compete will catapult you into the next level.

August 24

Love one another fervently with a pure heart.

1 Peter 1:22

Seek the ability to love with a pure heart. Love without judgement or prejudices. Have the grace to overlook the differences that we may have. When we love as God loves us it will bring so much purity to our lives.

August 25

May the Lord direct your hearts into the love of God

and into the steadfastness of Christ.

2 Thessalonians 3:5

When we allow God to have full control over our lives His will can be

accomplished. When we try to take control then we can delay any

blessings He has in store for us. Let God direct your story, He is the

perfect author.

August 26

My grace is sufficient for you, for power is perfected in

weakness.

2 Corinthians 12:9

Submitting to God allows Him to do the necessary work in our lives.

He wants us to rely on Him. He wants us to go to Him with our

weaknesses and allow Him to be our strength.. When we show Him that

we need Him, He will bring the blessings.

August 27

My times are in your hands.

Psalm 31:15

Even though we may like to decide when things happen in our lives, it is not up to us. God's timing is always perfect and only He knows just when to add or remove something from your life. Put your timing in His hands.

August 28

Rejoice in the Lord always; again I will say, rejoice.

Philippians 4:4

When you choose to have joy in your life you become like a walking advertisement for God's love. It's evident that He is present in your life because you are seeking the positives rather than letting anything negative bring you down. His light shines all around you.

August 29

He looks to the ends of the earth and sees everything

under the heavens.

Job 28:24

Man cannot build with his two hands what God has built. We are

capable of so many things here on earth but when you think about all

that God has created it makes you stand in awe of how amazing He

truly is.

August 30

If any of you lacks wisdom, let him ask of God who gives to all generously and without reproach, and it will be given to him.

James 1:5

God is in no hurry. When we try to rush ahead of His plans we may cause a delay or miss out on something better that He already had planned. When we wait on God, we can trust that He is fully working in our lives. We may not see what is happening but the inner work He is doing on us will prepare us for the blessings to come.

August 31

I have fought the good fight, I have finished the course, I have kept the faith.

2 Timothy 4:7

Tenacity in faith is a quality that helps people achieve their goals. That "never give up" attitude despite any of their circumstances will surely help them succeed. Be tenacious on your walk with Christ, He will be there to see you through it all.

September

September 1

Praise the name of the Lord your God, who has dealt wondrously with you.

Joel 2:26

Nothing in your life is a coincidence. Everything that happens in your life happens on purpose. God has decided every detail of your life. Be grateful for all of His blessings and every bit of those details.

September 2

Great is your faithfulness.

Lamentations 3:23

Remember that your troubles are only temporary. Even though it may

seem that they just go on and on, there is joy to come. Trust in the

good plans God has for your life for He is faithful and good.

September 3

Resist the enemy, stand firm in the faith, because you know the family of believers throughout the world is undergoing the same kind of sufferings.

1 Peter 5:9

The armor of God will shield you from the enemy. There is no doubt the enemy will try to attack you at your weakest moments. Stand firm in your faith and let God be your protector.

September 4

In the Lord I take refuge

Psalm 11:1

Each one of us has a place of protection in our lives. A place that will

keep us from all the dangers. Go to your God, let your spirit be filled

with Him, and know that He will protect you from harm. He is our

refuge.

September 5

He predestined us to adoption as sons through Jesus Christ to Himself, according to the kind intention of His will.

Ephesians 1:5

We are all born the same way into God's family. He is our Father and we are His children. Nothing in the exterior world matters according to Him because to Him we are all the same. Be conscious about treating each other this way.

September 6

Little children, let us not love with word or with tongue, but in deed and truth.

1 John 3:18

Putting the needs of others before our own is being loving in a selfless way. When we love like this we are glorifying God because this is the manner in which He loves us. Love others with actions not just with words.

September 7

He who began a good work in you will perfect it until

the day of Christ Jesus.

Philippians 1:6

God is not done yet. If you or a loved one is at a point where you feel

like things are standing still, don't give up hope. God will continue to

work in your life until everything is complete. He will keep all of His

promises to you.

September 8

I know that my Redeemer lives, and at the last He will

take His stand on earth.

Job 19:25

Nothing is ever absolute besides God Himself. He built an entire

world in six DAYS; He can certainly change your life in one. He is in

full control of everything, nothing is too difficult for Him. Hold onto the

hope that He will make a move in His timing.

September 9

I am the way the truth and the life.

John 14:6

There is no doubt. We must believe with all of our hearts, with all of our minds, and all of our souls that Jesus is Lord. He died on the cross and rose from the dead for us. He paid for our sins. Give thanks. There is no greater love than this. He is our way to eternal life.

September 10

Do not, therefore, fling away your fearless confidence, for it carries a great and glorious compensation go reward.

Hebrews 10:35

Don't let fear get in the way of accomplishing your goals. The enemy will try to intimidate you and convince you that you are not good enough, or you don't have the skills. Don't believe any of that. God will equip you with everything you need to make it happen.

September 11

For God is not the author of confusion, but of peace in

all the churches of the saints.

1 Corinthians 14:33

If you are in a situation where you are trying to make a decision and there is a lot of confusion surrounding it, then you can be sure that it is not coming from God. If it is for you, God will make a way. If it is not He will remove it.

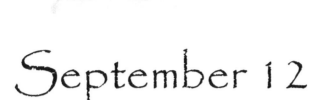

September 12

Behold, What I have seen to be good and fitting is for one to eat and drink, and to find enjoyment in all the labor in which he labors under the sun all the days which God gives him.

Ecclesiastes 5:18

It is our job to find the best in all we have and all we do. Things can have a way of becoming mundane sometimes but if we are willing to find joy in it and change it up a little, then something that is old can feel brand new.

September 13

But above all, my brethren, do not swear, either by heaven or by earth or by any other oath; but let you yes be a simple yes, and your no be a simple no, so that you may not sin and fall under condemnation.

James 5:12

When you have to make a decision about something whether big or small, check with God first. When you do that it will help you to be more decisive and simplify your answers. He will lead you in the right direction.

September 14

And the King will reply to them, Truly I tell you, in so far as you did if for one of the least of these My brethren, you did it for Me.

Matthew 25:40

God's voice is still and small. So sometimes it sounds like a whisper when he is asking us to do something. Listen to that voice. He is asking you to do it for a big reason, no matter how small it may seem.

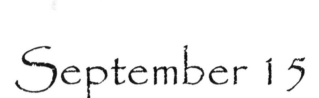

September 15

You shall assign to them as their responsibility all they

are to carry.

Numbers 4:27

We need to take responsibly for our own lives. God may bless us with

numerous things but it's up to us to take care of them. If we don't then it

will be nobody's fault but our own if we lose those blessings.

September 16

Here I am; send me.

Isaiah 6:8

Offer yourself to God and ask Him to use you according to His will. If you feel in your heart that God wants to use you in a big way, then pray for Him to guide you and equip you with the ability to make it happen.

September 17

Then I said to you, Dread not, neither be afraid of them.

Deuteronomy 1:29

Our attitude about how we approach things will make all the difference in the world. If we start something thinking it's going to be horrible then it probably will be. If we handle it with God and positive thinking then the outcome is going to be much better.

September 18

Pray that you may not enter into temptation.

Luke 22:40

Make sure to resist the devil at all times. He will try to push you as far as he can in your weakest moments. Remember that he has no control over you. God has the final say. Trust God to help you though your times of weakness.

September 19

For God speaks not only once, but more than once.

Job 33:14

There are going to be several times in your life when God id speaking

to you. Are you listening? It may not always be really obvious at first

but when you hear it multiple times you will know that it is God's voice

that you hear.

September 20

A humble spirit will obtain honor.

Proverbs 29:23

If God chooses to exalt you then you won't have to do any self promotion. Let God do His will and He will take care of the advancement. Live your life helping Him with the needs of others and glorifying Him and you will shine like a star.

September 21

Honor all people, love the brotherhood, fear God,

honor the King.

1 Peter 2:17

God knows what our motives are. If you are not doing things that honor

Him then He will not move you forward. If we do things with the same

selfless love He has for us then we are honoring Him.

September 22

Don't point your finger at someone else and try to pass the blame.

Hosea 4:4

Every person is responsible for their own actions. If someone did something that offended you and you react in a harsh way, it is on you to suffer the repercussions of that. If you chose to behave maturely then the outcome will be significantly different. Blame will not solve this issue.

September 23

Let each one as he has made up his own mind and purposed in his heart, not reluctantly or sorrowfully or under compulsion, for God loves a cheerful giver.

2 Corinthians 9:7

It brings God great joy to see one of His children being generous with others without expecting anything in return. It doesn't have to be something extremely expensive. If you are listening all around you will know the needs of others with just one small effort.

September 24

Pray at all times in the Spirit, with all prayer and

entreaty.

Ephesians 6:18

Prayer should be a daily practice. It forms a deeper relationship with

God. It should always start with thanksgiving and follow with a

conversation with God. It's not only about asking for what we need, it's

being grateful for what we already have.

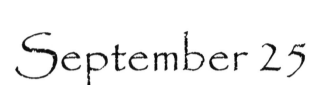

September 25

And when they heard it, lifted their voices together with

one united mind to God...

Acts 4:24

God wants us to come together. He does not want us to be divided.

We are meant to be unified in His name and following His ways. When

we do this then we can live peacefully together.

September 26

If we are thrown into the blazing furnace, the God we serve is able to deliver us from it, and he will deliver us from Your Majesty's hand.

Daniel 3:17

Things may look pretty bad right now but now more than ever we need to put our trust in Him. God is saying, You may walk through the fires but I will walk through them with you." Trust in Him!

September 27

I will give them one heart and I will put a new spirit within them; and I will take the stony heart out of their flesh and will give them a heart of flesh.

Ezekiel 11:19

It is ok to have emotions. That is how God made us. When you are feeling like you are overwhelmed by your emotions then you can ask God to help you manage them. It's ok to feel how you do just don't stay on that one thing for too long. Have the emotion then let it go.

September 28

Having eyes, do you not see, and having ears, do you not hear and perceive and understand the sense of what is said? And do you not remember?

Mark 8:18

We need to make an effort to see and hear things in the manner that God would. Lots of times we get caught up in our own perception of how things are based on our past experiences. WE need to take a step back and really listen and receive things in a more positive way.

September 29

For the thing which I greatly fear comes upon me, and

that of which I am afraid befalls me.

Job 3:25

The enemy will use our fears against us. He will use that opportunity to

keep us down. It is our job in those times to turn to God and ask for

His support. He is our source of strength and will get us through

anything. Don't let your fears keep you in bondage.

September 30

For My yoke is wholesome and my burden is light and

easy to be borne.

Matthew 11:30

This scripture is about being able to discern God's voice. When it is

not from Him you will feel rushed and confused and panicked. When it

is from Him you will feel at ease with a sense of peace. Trust in that still

small voice.

October

October 1

Psalm 42:1

As the deer pants for streams of water, so my soul pants for you, O God.

Our desire for God needs to be above all things. When we are seeking outside sources to fulfill us it leaves us feeling like something is missing. When we fill our lives with God we will keep ourselves feeling full.

October 2

He knows to refuse the evil and chose the good.

Isaiah 7:15

This is something that should become automatic. When we know God and His spirit and His ways then it should be like second nature to chose the good over evil. The choice of good will lift you up and evil will tear you down. Your choice!

October 3

Strive to enter by the narrow door for many, I tell you,

will try to enter and will not be able.

Luke 13:24

Yes, the narrow path is definitely not the easiest, but if you are willing

to push trough and make strong efforts, the reward will be greater than

you've imagined. God will be there with you every step of the way.

October 4

It is the Lord Who examines and judges me.

1 Corinthians 4:4

There is always going to be someone who will criticize you about something. Here is the good news. You don't need to accept that criticism. Stand firm in who you are with God and offer up that judgment to God, then say a little prayer for your critic.

October 5

Let there be no strife, I beg of you, between you and me, or between your herdsman and my herdsman.

Genesis 13:8

If you are busy helping other people with their needs, then God is gonna get busy attending to your needs. It's that simple. God helps those who help others. Don't hold your possessions too tightly because you could lose them anyway.

October 6

For I will forgive their iniquity, and I will remember their

sin no more.

Jeremiah 31:34

God keeps no record of past wrongdoings. When you are asking Him

for forgiveness then you need to let it go at the same time. That does't

mean to keep repeating the same sin over and over because God

forgave you. It means you need to truly repent and commit to turning

away from sin.

October 7

Having gifts that differ according to the grace given us,

let us use them...

Romans 12:6

We all are born with spiritual gifts. Do you know what your gift is? If so, How are you using it to glorify God? God made you for a very specific purpose. You are responsible for using the gifts He gave you in a manner that will serve Him well.

October 8

Hear, O our God, for we are despised. Turn their taunts upon their own heads and give then for a prey in a land of their captivity.

Nehemiah 4:4

Keep your eyes on God and the job He called you to do. Don't let any distractions get in your way. The more you practice this the more you will know what the distractions are. Don't give the enemy a chance to attack. Focus, focus, focus!

October 9

Beloved, I pray that you may prosper in every way and may keep well, even as your soul keeps well and prospers.

3 John 1:2

To prosper doesn't just mean to earn money or acquire a bunch of material things. You can prosper by filling your life with positive experiences. Things that affirm your faith and give you a feeling of completeness. God's way will fill your soul.

October 10

Get ready; be prepared...

Ezekiel 38:7

God has something very specific in store for you. Are you ready for what He has planned? Things don't always happen in our timing but in the wait we must be doing our part to prepare for what is about to happen.

October 11

Let your eyes look straight ahead; fix your gaze directly

before you.

Proverbs 4:25

You can't change any of the mistakes you've made in the past. All you

can do is learn from them and decide to make better choices in the

future. Don't keep looking behind you. Look straight ahead, with your

eyes fixed on Christ, and choose better.

October 12

Not by might, nor by power, but by My Spirit...

Zechariah 4:6

God has anointed you with the Holy Spirit to help you in all you do.

When we are full of THE SPIRIT it helps us to stay at peace and

allows us to minister to others. It is God's strength within us that make

us strong enough each day.

October 13

Because of our faith in Him, we dare to have boldness

of free access.

Ephesians 3:12

Trust in who God created you to be. He wants you to be the best

version of yourself. We can increase our confidence by knowing that

the reason He created us serves a great purpose. There is only one

you. Be you.

October 14

And Jesus said to them, The Sabbath was made on account and for the sake of man...

Mark 2:27

A resting day is a necessary day. If we don't take the time for ourselves to recharge our batteries then complete exhaustion is sure to follow. Take a day, put your feet up, relax, and recharge. All the work will still be there tomorrow.

October 15

And He said to them, "Come after Me, follow Me, and

I will make you fishers of men."

Matthew 4:19

The timing is not always gonna be favorable when God is calling you to

do something. It is up to you to stop and listen and obey. How do you

know if your prayers are going to be answered if you're not willing to

take the next step?

October 16

Then shall your light break forth like the morning sun...

Isaiah 58:8

If you want to be a true expression of God's light then you should start by helping others. There is nothing that makes God's love shine more brightly than a selfless person. Be the giver more than the receiver, and God will satisfy your every need.

October 17

Invoke blessings upon and pray for the happiness of those who curse you, implore God's blessings upon those who abuse you.

Luke 6:28

There is going to come a time where you will need to forgive someone who has hurt you. Depending on the offense, it may take several times to forgive them. Real spiritual growth happens when we can pray for their well being as well as forgiving them.

October 18

Let those who are wise understand these things. Let those with discernment listen carefully. The paths of the Lord are true and right, and righteous people live by walking in them.

Hosea 14:9

When we listen carefully we can understand what God is trying to tell us. If we want to live according to God's will and avoid a lot of unnecessary struggles, then we need to stay in prayer and ask God to increase our discernment.

October 19

The Wicked flee when no man purses them, but the righteous are bold as a lion.

Proverbs 28:1

Even if we are naturally meek in manner we can still be bold on the inside. God is the source of our strength and when we use that strength in our ENDEAVORS, nothing that comes against us will ever prevail.

October 20

I am speaking the truth in Christ. I am not lying; my

conscience by the Holy Spirit bearing witness with

me...

Romans 9:1

Are you really being your true authentic self? Nobody is perfect and

they are not expected to be. Why do we portray ourselves differently

than who we really are? The only acceptance we need is from God. He

loves us exactly as we are. Be authentically you!

October 21

I can press on, that I may lay hold of that for which

Jesus Christ has also laid hold of me.

Philippians 3:12

We belong to Christ. Our lives need to be a reflection of this. It's not about the plans that we make for ourselves, it's making sure we are following the plans He has laid out for us.

October 22

Come up here, and I will show you things which must take place...

Revelations 4:1

It is important to keep striving to level up. Keep reaching to meet a better version of yourself. We will be in line with the standards of God when our lives are completely filled with Him and practicing His Word.

October 23

I was not disobedient to the heavenly vision.

Acts 26:19

When we stay obedient to the heavenly vision of God, we are allowing Him to do the necessary work in our lives. We have to make a commitment to this walk with Him in order to bear fruit. Before trees can bear their fruit they need lots of water and light. Take care of your tree of life.

October 24

"Preach the word!"

2 Timothy 4:2

To be a disciple of God he is asking us to preach His word. This is not just a one time event. This is a daily commitment to spreading God's holy message. The determination to speak God's truth will help to liberate you and the people you are ministering it to.

October 25

"Do you love Me?"

John 21:17

Jesus asks this question of Peter and we must ask ourselves the same.

How are you showing Jesus that you love Him? His display of love for

us could not be more evident. Show Jesus how much you love Him by

following His ways.

October 26

He went out not knowing where he was going.

Hebrews 11:8

This is the ultimate test of faith. Will you go where God is leading you even if you don't know where you are going? We are to walk by faith not by sight. God will lead us to the right place for us.

October 27

My earnest expectation and hope that in nothing I shall be ashamed, but with all boldness, as always, so now also Christ will be magnified in my body, whether by life or by death.

Philippians 1:20

We can expect to have many things in our lives, but the truth is, without completely surrendering your life to our Lord, you won't be able to live your best life possible. You have Christ in you. Let His ways shine brightly through you.

October 28

When I saw Him, I fell at His feet as dead.

Revelations 4:17

God reveals Himself to you in many ways. There is something about this image that inspires awe. If He were standing right in front of you I imagine you wouldn't even be able to look directly at Him. Seek Him, find Him, stand in awe.

October 29

Judge not, that you be not judged.

Matthew 7:1

If you don't want others to be critical of you then you should not be critical of others. We have one judge and jury and it is up to Him to make the necessary corrections in us. Pray for God to help you see as He sees.

October 30

You call Me Teacher and Lord, and you say well, for so am I.

John 13:13

The level of your growth depends on your level of faith. What are you allowing the Lord our God to teach you? There are lessons in every aspect of our lives. You have a choice. Will you let Him show you the way?

October 31

Let patience have its perfect work, that you may be

perfect and complete, lacking nothing.

James 1:4

Patience is a virtue. Sometimes we will have to wait when it comes to our

goals and aspirations. God may put something on our hearts but that

doesn't mean it will happen right away. It's what you do in the wait that

matters.

November

November 1

He would not drink it but poured it out to the Lord.

2 Samuel 23:16

The Lord will add many blessings to your life. It's up to you to maximize those blessings. He doesn't want you to just hoard them for yourselves. He wants you to share those blessings with others.

November 2

We have renounced the hidden things of shame.

2 Corinthians 4:2

The hidden things of shame are the things that we are thinking about that we don't want anyone else to know about. These are the things that we should be renouncing. They are not in line with the light of God. Ask God to help you release these thoughts.

November 3

He said to them, "This kind can come out by nothing but prayer and fasting."

Mark 9:29

Your continual concentration on Jesus Christ will bring you through any situation that you may face. Nothing we are facing is too much for Him to handle. Rely on Him, pray for His wisdom and strength and He will provide.

November 4

But you, beloved, building yourselves up on your most

holy faith and praying in the Holy Spirit.

Jude 20

The way we can continue to grow is to feed our relationship with God.

The more we add His ways to our lives the more we can experience His

love through us. Continue to read the Bible and study His truth. He

will feed your soul.

November 5

Stand fast therefore in the liberty by which Christ has made us free.

Galatians 5:1

God made us free for a reason. You can't force your beliefs on someone else. You can educate them based on what you know but God wants them to seek Him out in their own timing. Be patient and kind and lead by example.

November 6

I now rejoice in my sufferings for you and fill up in my flesh what is lacking in the afflictions of Christ.

Colossians 1:24

The areas of our lives that are lacking is where we need to replace with Christ. Our flesh sometimes will seek out things that are not healthy for us. We need to recognize what those areas are and replace them with something that is more Christ like.

November 7

When they were alone, He explained all things to His disciples.

Mark 4:34

It is important to spend time alone with God. He wants to have a relationship with you. Spending time alone will help you to really listen to what God is asking you to do. When you're listening, He's explaining.

November 8

Indeed the hour is coming...that you will be scattered...

John 16:32

The world can be a very busy place. It can be very easy to get lost in all the distractions. The one thing that we don't want to turn away from is our LORD. Make sure that you are never far from Him and He will draw closer to you.

November 9

Have mercy on us, O, Lord, have mercy on us! For we are exceedingly filled with contempt.

Psalm 123:2

God is always willing to forgive us when we are asking for it. To truly repent you must turn away from that sin and work really hard not to repeat the same offense. God is a God of mercy. We have to make the effort to follow His ways.

November 10

Take up the whole armor of God...

Ephesians 6:13

There is no greater protector than God Himself. He is your shield through any troubles you may have. God wants to know that you need Him. Go to Him and He will be your provider.

November 11

I will very gladly spend and be spent for your souls...

2 Corinthians 12:15

It is better to spend a lifetime with Christ than to spend a lifetime alone.

He has paid the price for our sins. What price are you willing to pay to

help others? Our souls are bought and paid for because of Him.

Couldn't we make the effort to do His will?

November 12

I set My rainbows in the cloud, and it shall be for the

sign of the covenant between Me and the earth.

Genesis 9:13

Are you the type of person that needs a sign before you act on

something? There are lots of ways that God will give us a sign in nature

or in a song or even through another human being. That is not always

going to be the case. He still wants us to have faith in the things we

have not seen.

November 13

Whatever I tell you in the dark, speak in the light; and what you hear in the ear, preach on the housetops.

Matthew 10:27

We all are going to experience dark times at some point in our lives. Sometimes God will intentionally put us there to teach us something. It is our job to be the light in those hours of darkness. Tell people who your God is.

November 14

Which of you, intending to build a tower, does not sit down first and count the cost, whether he has enough to finish it...?

Luke 14:28

God wants us to keep moving forward no matter how things may seem on the outside. What He started in us He wants to finish. The only one we need to check in with is Him. He makes all things possible according to His will.

November 15

By one offering He has perfected forever those who

are being sanctified.

Hebrews 10:14

God has restored us Himself by the sacrifice of His only Son. We are

sanctified because of this sacrifice. The more grateful we are for this

offering and sacrifice, the better we can understand who God is.

November 16

Christ did not send me to baptize, but to preach the

gospel...

1 Corinthians 1:17

All God really wants us to do is share. Share everything about Him

and His word. We are only human, with many imperfections. He is not

asking us to be perfect but to share His perfect love.

November 17

They said to Moses, "You speak with us, and we will hear; but let not God speak with us, lest we die."

Exodus 20:19

This is about when we are deliberately being disobedient to God. We'd rather listen to someone else than check in with Him. People don't know what God knows. He's the Father that we want to answer to.

November 18

I will give your life to you as a prize in all places,

wherever you go.

Jeremiah 45:5

In order to have true oneness with God you have to be willing to release your own ideas and inhibitions. He wants you to surrender to His will completely. When you trust in His ways He will then reward you for your faithfulness.

November 19

Look at the birds of the air... Consider the lilies of the field...

Matthew 6:26,28

God has created all these things. When you are having doubts, consider these things. He helped the birds to fly, and the flowers to grow. If He can make these things happen, then He can certainly do amazing things in your life. Trust in Him.

November 20

If the Son makes you free, you shall be free indeed.

John 8:36

Jesus ha s set us free. We should have an eternal debt of gratitude towards Him for His sacrifice for us. Freedom does not mean that we should have no consequences for our actions, it means we are free to choose.

November 21

Those who are Christ's have crucified the flesh with its passions and desires.

Galatians 5:24

We are to abandon the sinful ways of the world. It's not going to be easy. It has to be a daily choice to avoid the temptations. God will be our strength to endure these challenges but we have to keep choosing the next right thing.

November 22

I did not come to bring peace but a sword.

Matthew 10:34

There are times that God will have to come down on us harshly. There is always a lesson to be learned in our suffering. It is just as a parent needs to discipline their child in order to teach them right from wrong. It is difficult but necessary.

November 23

By the grace of God I am what I am and His grace

toward me was not in vain...

1 Corinthians 15:10

God has given us so much grace. We don't DESERVE ALL the

things He has done for us. He has a very good reason for creating us

each uniquely and has a specific purpose for all of us. Be sure to thank

Him for everything that you are and all that you have because without

Him we are nothing.

November 24

Rise let us be going.

Matthew 26:46

There are going to be moments of despair in our lives. Moments that

we are going to need to take a stand and rise above our circumstances.

Nothing in this world will help us get there better than God. He will lift

you up out of the ashes.

November 25

If you will return, O Israel, says the Lord...

Jeremiah 4:1

Even if we slip and turn away from God for a little while, He never leaves us and He welcomes us to return to Him at any time. As long as we are going to Him He is there waiting for us with open arms.

November 26

We make it our aim... to be well pleasing to Him.

2 Corinthians 5:9

Our number one priority should be how well we love our Lord. Loving Him is not only about our relationship with Him but also about our relationships with others. Are we treating people with kindness and respect? Are we giving selflessly? These are just a few of the things we can do to please Him.

November 27

People's own foolishness ruins their lives, but in their

minds they blame the Lord.

Proverbs 19:3

Blaming others can beat down your soul until it becomes

unrecognizable. We need to take responsibility for our own actions.

Own up to the problem and ask God to help you fix it. No matter what

happens you can always move forward with God.

November 28

The people had a mind to work.

Nehemiah 4:6

When you have your work ethic set straight, you are going to be more likely to soar. You can't just sit around and wait for God to do it all for you. You have to put in your share and then He will show you more.

November 29

Those of us who are strong and believe the faith need to step in and lend a hand to those who falter... Each one of us needs to look at the good of the people around us, asking ourselves,

"How can I help?"

Romans 15:1-2

Be a willing helper! When you are helping others you will feel an emotional charge beyond explanation. The feeling you get is better than anything you could ever ask for. I think it is God's gift back to you for being generous.

November 30

Encourage one another and build each other up as you

are already doing.

1 Thessalonians 5:11

Being an encourager is one of the spiritual gifts from God. If you know

that you were granted this gift then you should do everything in your

power to use it daily. Making others feel better about themselves will

not only lift their spirits but will also lift yours.

December

December 1

He gives power to the weak, and to those who have no

might He increases strength.

Isaiah 40:29

God loves to give the unlikely person an opportunity. He is not looking

fo what is on the outside, He looks for how a person uses their heart.

He will increase the strength of that person so that they may fulfill His

will.

December 2

Applying all diligence, in your faith supply moral

excellence.

2 Peter 1:5

Living a life of integrity will help to develop a person's character.

Character is something that can continue to build throughout your life.

Apply God's truth to your character and you r life will be filled with

blessings.

December 3

God doesn't want us to be shy with His gifts, but bold

and loving and sensible.

2 Timothy 1:7

God wants us to step outside of our comfort zones. No major

accomplishments ever got done by standing still. He wants us to take

risks in our faith and trust that what He is asking us to do will work out

for the best.

December 4

Step out of the traffic. Take a long, loving look at Me, and High God, above politics, above everything.

Psalm 46:10

God is above all things. You need to put Him first in your life in order to live the life He designed for you. When you search for answers in worldly things you will not find what you are looking for.

December 5

A good person's words will help many others.

Proverbs 10:21

Treating others with kindness should be at the top of your list. It takes no effort at all to treat others with respect. It could change someone's life for the better if we are giving them some encouragement. Be the person that builds someone up not tears them down.

December 6

There are many rooms in my Father's house; I would not tell you this if it were not true. I am going there to prepare a place for you.

John 14:2

Can you imagine what it would be like to have a room in heaven with God? I imagine it would be something that you couldn't possibly fully absorb. Death is not something to fear but rather a welcome home from our Father.

December 7

God created great sea creatures and every living thing that scurries and swarms in the water, and every sort of bird-each producing offspring of the same kind. And God saw that it was good.

Genesis 1:21

God has created this world and everything in it. Every detail is because of Him. Take a moment to consider all the beautiful things there really are. The blue sky, the deep ocean, the color of a bird, the size of a lion, every bit of it is for a reason all to serve a purpose.

December 8

Whatever you do, work heartily, as for the Lord and

not for men.

Colossians 3:23

There are a lot of things that we have to do in our lives that won't bring

much enjoyment on a typical day. If we say a prayer of thanksgiving as

we are doing them it will help to change our mindset from dread into

peaceful. If you didn't have laundry to wash you would have no clothes

to wear.

December 9

Indeed, by faith our ancestors received approval.

Hebrews 11:2

Ask God to help you live in a way that pleases Him and makes Him proud. Just as we are children that want to please our parents, we should be aiming to please God. Anything we do now will pave the way for any family that comes after us.

December 10

"Put your sword back in its place," Jesus said to him, "For all who draw the sword will die by the sword. Do you think I cannot call on my Father, and He will at once put at my disposal more than twelve legions of angels?"

Matthew 26:52-53

There may be a time in your life that you will need to restrain yourself from a fight with another person. This isn't just a physical FIGHT; it could also be an argument. Try to have more godly behavior and ask God for His help when you need it.

December 11

Each of us shall give account of himself to God.

Romans 14:12

Increase your standard and hold yourself accountable in God's eyes.
Not just with your actions but with your thoughts also. Level up your
life and strive to honor God and the Kingdom of Heaven.

December 12

If either of them falls down, one can help the other up.

But pity anyone who falls and has no one to help them

up.

Ecclesiastes 4:10

We all should be helping each other. That is one of the main reasons

why God created us. It brings Him great joy to see His children doing

His work. If we are seeking help then we should consider who needs

help around us.

December 13

Your wife will be like a fruitful grapevine, flourishing within your home. Your children will be like vigorous olive trees as they sit around your table.

Psalm 128:3

We need to make sure that we are expressing gratitude towards the relationships we have in our lives. Don't just worry about the things that bring you stress, consider the love that they bring to you and you bring to them. Ask God to bless those relationships.

December 14

Do not be fooled: "Bad friends will ruin good habits."

1 Corinthians 15:33

You have to be very careful about the company you keep. Sometimes the enemy will put someone in your life that will try to distract you from the will of God and His purpose. Even family can cause you to be tempted and compromise your calling. Ask God to help you break free of these temptations and surround you with more believers.

December 15

Keep a good conscience so that in the thing in which you are slandered, those who revile your good behavior in Christ will be put to shame.

1 Peter 3:16

Do everything with integrity. If your conscience is free from bad behaviors then any criticism someone may have about you will never hold water. God's light will shine through you and no one will ever believe those lies.

December 16

"The foreigner residing among you must be treated as your native-born. Love them as yourself, for you were foreigners in Egypt. I am the Lord your God."

Leviticus 19:34

Every blessing we have is from God. He wants us to share those blessings with other people. Don't be too stingy with what you have because it all could be taken away in a minute. Hearts are meant to be shared with each other. Make them available.

December 17

He delivers the needy when they call, the poor and

those who have no helper.

Psalm 72:12

Some people will suffer more than we could possibly imagine. Some

more than others. People who don't know God, even some who do, may

feel a sense of hopelessness. Take a moment to say a prayer for those

people so there may be some light in their darkness.

December 18

"If anyone slaps you on the cheek, offer him the other cheek, too. If someone takes your coat, do not stop him from taking your shirt too."

Luke 6:29

Have you ever been kind to the unkind or loved the unloveable? It's easy to show kindness and love to someone who gives those things in return. Try giving those things to someone you know who cannot repay you. Ask God to heal their hearts from their pain.

December 19

Do not throw away your confidence which has a great

reward.

Hebrews 10:35

Do you have Godfidence in your life? Yes, I know this isn't an actual

word but I like to think of it as a word to replace confidence. Because

only with God can we truly have the confidence to accomplish anything.

December 20

I bow my knees before the Father, from whom every

family in heaven and on the earth is named.

Ephesians 3:14-15

There is nothing that God would not do for His children. He is our

Father and our protector. Give Him thanks and praise for the family

He has brought us into. Live in gratitude for all the sacrifices He has

made for us.

December 21

The very hairs on your head are all numbered.

Matthew 10:30

Let God's love for you humble you. His love is so big that He accounted for every single detail about you when He created you. Glorify Him in all you do because everything He has done has been for you.

December 22

"Go your way, eat the fat and drink sweet wine and

send portions of them to those for whom nothing is

prepared, for this day is holy to our Lord; and do not

be grieved, for the joy of the Lord is your strength."

Nehemiah 8:10

There are going to be days when things seem dark but you have to

focus on the positives. Give thanks for what you do have and then

share those things with others. Someone always has it worse than you

do so in bringing joy to them your life willed be filled with light.

December 23

All Scripture is given by inspiration of God, and is profitable for doctrine, for reproof, for correction, for instruction in righteousness.

2 Timothy 3:16

Let God be the source of your inspiration. Make a conscience choice to seek His will and let Him lead you on His path. Ask Him to show you the things He wants you to see and hear. Let His example be one that you emulate.

December 24

Every valley shall be raised up, every mountain and hill

made low; the rough ground shall become level, the

rugged places in a plain.

Isaiah 40:4

Every time you lose your way you have to look to the best navigator of

all. Your God will not steer you in the wrong direction. He will make

your crooked path straight. Trust in His guidance because the road to

His love is always the best traveled.

December 25

"Martha, Martha," the Lord answered, "you are worried and upset about many things, but few things are needed-or indeed only one. Mary has chosen what is better, and it will not be taken away from her."

Luke 10:41-42

We have to keep our eyes looking up to Christ. He is number one in our lives. He is the one thing that could never be taken away. You can cling to Him and He will comfort you. Nothing comes before HIM; no worries will matter in the end. He was born to save.

December 26

I fear, lest somehow, as the serpent deceived Eve by his craftiness, so your minds may be corrupted from the simplicity that is in Christ.

2 Corinthians 11:3

Don't let the idea that you need more drive you away from what God wants you to have. It is the most simple thing, LOVE. Love is all you need to increase blessings in your life. Give big love and you will receive big love.

December 27

All my longings lie open before you, Lord; my sighing is

not hidden from you.

Psalm 38:9

Leave everything to God. All your disappointments, all your sorrows,

all your dreams, and every tomorrow. Everything is in His hands to take

care of. Nothing is too difficult for Him. When we rely on Him, He will

fulfill every promise He made.

December 28

No temptation has overtaken you except such as is common to man; but God is faithful, who will not allow you to be tempted beyond what you are able, but with temptation will also make the way of escape, that you may be able to bear it.

1 Corinthians 10:13

God is not gonna give you anything you can't handle. It might seem like it's too much sometimes but that is just a test of your faith. He wants you to go to Him with any of your struggles or weaknesses and ask Him to be your strength.

December 29

"You don't have enough faith," Jesus told them. "I tell youth truth, if you had faith even as small as a mustard seed, you could say to this mountain, 'Move from here to there,' and it would move. Nothing would be impossible."

Matthew 17:20

With God all things are possible. If you only believe just a little bit, then there is potential for growth from there. Think about the size of the mustard seed and the size of the tree that grows from that one tiny seed. Your faith has endless possibilities.

December 30

"Build up, build up, prepare the road! Remove the

obstacles out of the way of my people."

Isaiah 57:14

When you clear your heart from all the negatively and the doubt and

continue with faith in your Lord, He will clear the obstacles from your

life. He can move any mountain and He can wash away your sins and

make you clean again.

December 31

"Why do you call me good?" Jesus asked. "Only God is truly good."

Mark 10:18

Only God is perfection. Even Jesus never considered Himself to be the same despite all His good works. Humble yourself to this notion because only God is absolute. There is no love bigger than His.

About the Author

Rhode Island native and author Missy Ducharme has a passion for giving back and helping others. Strong in faith, she strives to bring encouragement, strength and healing in everything she writes.

Missy lives a very full life. She is raising her daughter Juliet, runs a successful salon, Imagine This Day Spa, and performs as a singer/songwriter to benefit Boston Children's Hospital and Musicians On Call.

Missy has been writing since childhood but was inspired to write songs after the loss of her first daughter Emma Rose. She felt called to write this book because in her experience, her faith helped her through some of the most difficult times. She hopes this book will serve as a bridge between you and God.

About JEBWizard Publishing

JEBWizard Publishing offers a hybrid approach to publishing. By taking a vested interest in the success of your book, we put our reputation on the line to create and market a quality publication. We offer a customized solution based on your individual project needs.

Our catalog of authors spans the spectrum of fiction, non-fiction, Young Adult, True Crime, Self-help, and Children's books.

Contact us for submission guidelines at

https://www.jebwizardpublishing.com

Info@jebwizardpublishing.com

Or in writing at

JEBWizard Publishing

37 Park Forest Rd.

Cranston, RI 02920

CPSIA information can be obtained
at www.ICGtesting.com
Printed in the USA
FSHW022146250221
78922FS